W9-BDX-155

YOU CAN TEACH YOURSELF®

UKE

by William Bay

This book is available either by itself or packaged with a companion audio and/or video recording. If you have purchased the book only, you may wish to purchase the recordings separately. The publisher strongly recommends using a recording along with the text to assure accuracy of interpretation and make learning easier and more enjoyable.

CD CONTENTS

1 2 3 4 5 6 7 8 9 0

Visit us on the Web at www.melbay.com — E-mail us at email@melbay.com

Contents

How To Hold The Uke

Standing

REMEMBER TO:
1 Hold the uke above your waist.
2 Hold it at a slight upward angle.
3 Use your right forearm to press
   the uke against your body.
4 Relax!

Sitting

Parts Of The Uke

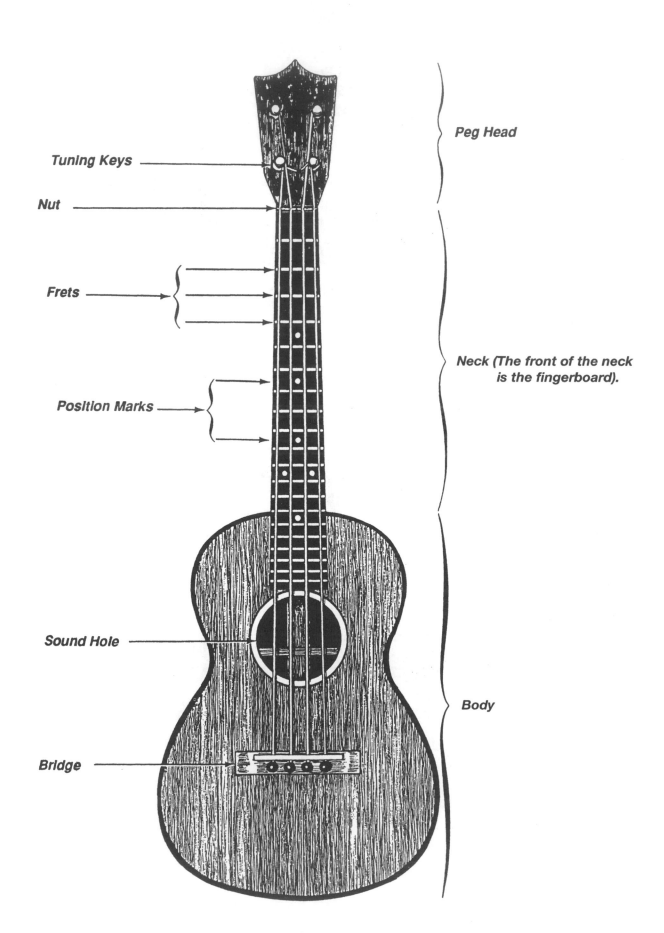

Peg Head

Tuning Keys

Nut

Frets

Position Marks

Neck (The front of the neck is the fingerboard).

Sound Hole

Body

Bridge

Ways To Tune Your Uke

1. Tune It To A Piano

This method will use *"C tuning."* In C tuning the strings are tuned to the following notes:

First String . . . . A ①
Second String . . . . . . E ②
Third String . . . . C ③
Fourth String . . . . . . G ④

On a piano the notes are found as follows:

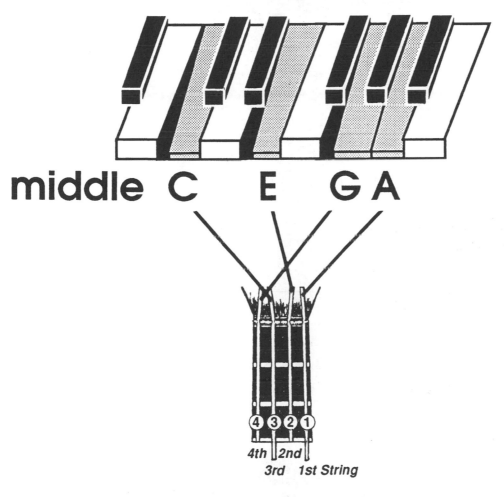

middle **C** **E** **G A**

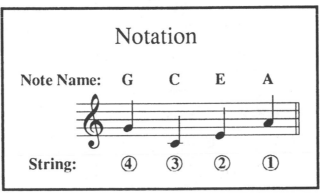

Notation

Note Name:	G	C	E	A
String:	④	③	②	①

2. Tuning With A Pitch Pipe

Ukulele pitch pipes can be purchased from most music stores. Blow into the appropriate sound hole and tune the string to the correct pitch.

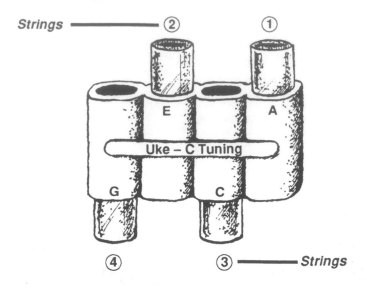

3. Tuning By Ear

Once you tune your first string to a pitch that sounds correct (not too high or too low), you can use the following expression:

	My	dog	has	fleas.
Note:	G	C	E	A
String:	④	③	②	①

Important Hint

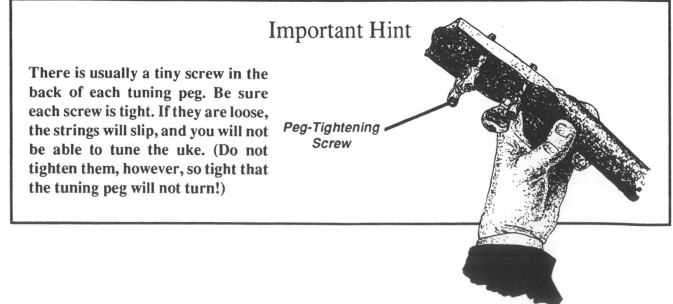

There is usually a tiny screw in the back of each tuning peg. Be sure each screw is tight. If they are loose, the strings will slip, and you will not be able to tune the uke. (Do not tighten them, however, so tight that the tuning peg will not turn!)

Peg-Tightening Screw

Strumming Your Uke

1. Using A Pick

Picks can be purchased at your local music store. It is usually desirable to use a "felt" pick. This will give your uke a soft, mellow tone. Plastic picks will give a sharper, more brittle tone. If a plastic pick is to be used, try to find a thin, very flexible one.

Felt Pick

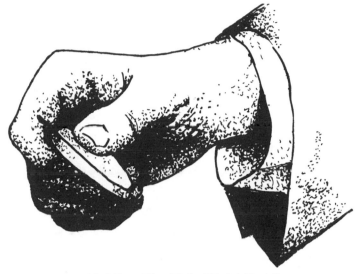

Holding The Pick (Right Hand)

2. Using Your Thumb

You can also strum your uke with your right-hand thumb.

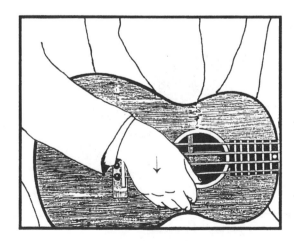

Down Strum ↓

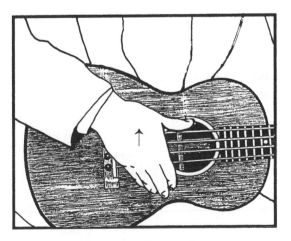

Up Strum ↑

The Left Hand

The following illustrations show the proper positioning of the left hand. Notice that only the *tips* of the left-hand fingers are used to press down the strings. (Be sure your fingers do not accidentally touch the adjacent string. If this happens, the adjacent string will sound muffled or deadened.) Be sure the thumb is on the back of the neck, *not* wrapped around the side. Finally, when you press down a string, place your finger behind the metal fret, *not* on top of it.

Correct

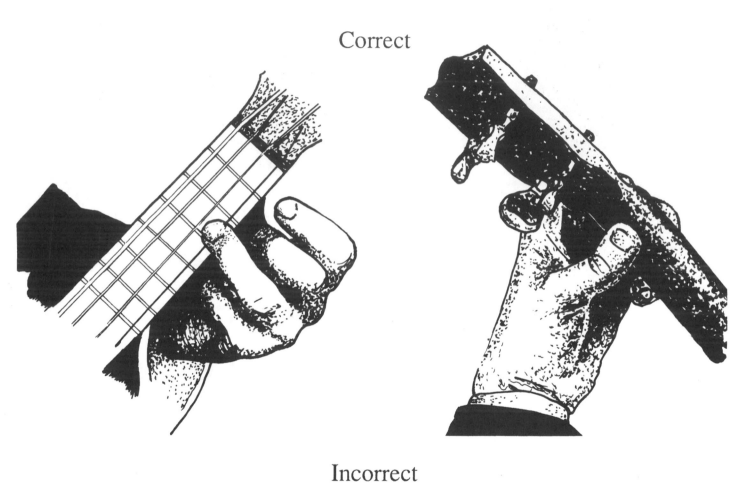

Incorrect

How To Read Chord Diagrams

A chord diagram shows you where to place your fingers in order to play a chord. The vertical lines are the strings. The horizontal lines are the frets. The circled numbers are left-hand fingers.

Left-hand fingers are numbered as follows:

Our First Chord
C

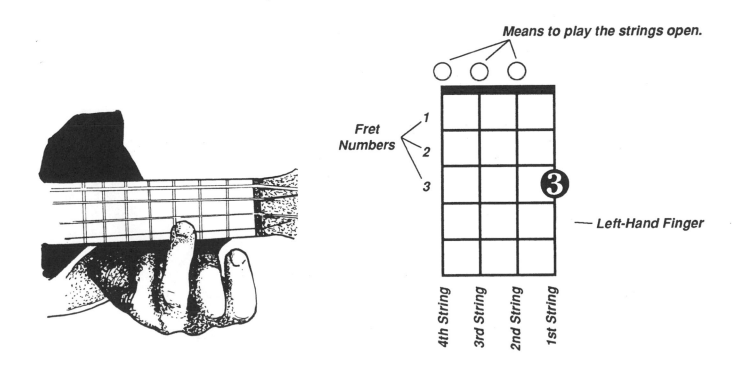

Playing The C Chord

Practice strumming the C chord until it sounds clear.

Time Signatures

Every song has a time signature. The time signature appears at the beginning of every song and tells you how many beats or counts are in each measure.

$\frac{4}{4}$ or $\mathbb{C}$ = "Common Time"

Hold the C chord and play as follows.

Remember: / = Down Strum

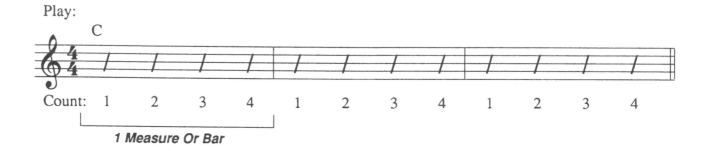

$\frac{3}{4}$ = Three-Four Or "Waltz" Time

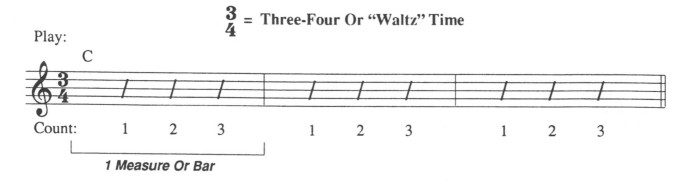

$\frac{2}{4}$ = Two-Four Or "March" Time

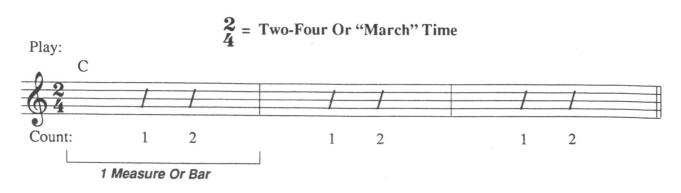

Our First Songs

Reading Music

Three Blind Mice

Row, Row, Row Your Boat

A New Chord

G7

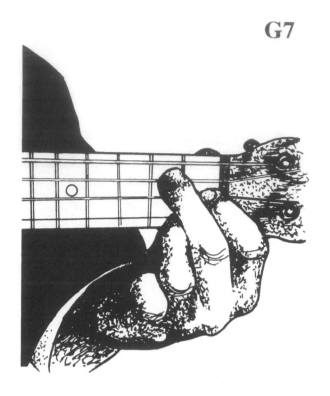

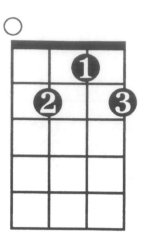

Starting pitch

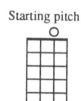

Skip To My Lou

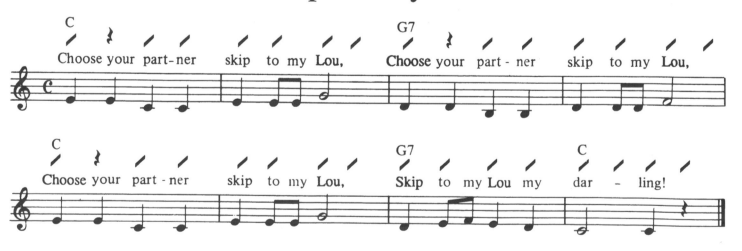

C
Left and Right,   Oh skip to my Lou
C
Left and Right,   Oh skip to my Lou

G7
Left and Right,   Oh skip to my Lou
G7   C
Skip to my Lou my darling.

Rock-A-My Soul

Polly Wolly Doodle

13

Oh, My Darling Clementine

Starting pitch

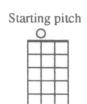

In a cav - ern in a can - yon ex - ca - va - ting for a

mine - Dwelt a min - er, for- ty nin - er and his daugh-ter Clem- en - tine.

Oh my dar - ling, oh my dar - ling, oh my dar - ling Clem - en -

tine, - You are lost and gone for - ev - er I am sor - ry Clem en - tine.

14

Three Fishermen

Starting pitch

1. Once **there** were three fish - er — men.

Once **there** were three fish - er — men. Fish-er, Fish-er, men, men, men.

Fish - er, Fish-er men, men, men. Once **there** were three Fish - er — men.

vs. 2. First one's name was Abraham
(Repeat)
Abra, Abra, ham, ham, ham
(Repeat)
First one's name was Abraham

vs. 4. Third one's name was Jacob
Jakey, Jakey, cub, cub, cub.

vs. 3. Second's name was Isaac.
Isy, Isy, ac, ac, ac.

vs. 5. Wish **they'd** gone to Amsterdam.
Amster, Amster, dam, dam, dam.

Pay Me Money Down

Starting pitch

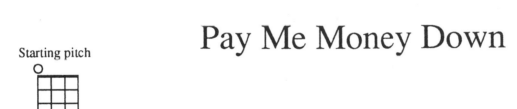

West Indian Folk Song

Chorus Pay me,_ oh, pay me,_ Pay me my mon-ey down,_

Pay me or go to jail,_ Pay me my mon-ey down._

2. I thought I heard the captain say,
Pay me my money down.
Tomorrow is our sailing day,
Pay me my money down.
Chorus

Oh Where Has My Little Dog Gone?

It Ain't Gonna Rain No More!

Down-Up Strum

/ = Down Strum
V = Up Strum

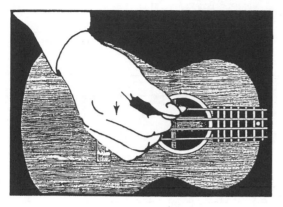

Down Strum /

Up Strum V

Buffalo Gals

Starting pitch

Strum	Down	Down	up	Down	up	Down	up

C
/ V / V / V / V   / V / V / V / V   G7 / V / V / V / V   C / V / V / V / V
I was walk-ing down the street, down the street, down the street a

/ V / V / V / V   / V / V / V / V   G7 / V / V / V / V   C / V / V / V / V
hand-some gal I chanced to meet oh she was fair to see.

/ V / V / V / V   / V V / V / V   G7 / V V / V / V   C / V V / V / V
Buf-fa-lo gals won't-cha come out to-nite, come out to-nite, come out to-nite,

/ V / V / V / V   / V V / V / V   G7 / V / V / V / V   C / V / V / V / V
Buf-fa-lo gals won't-cha come out to-nite and dance by the light of the moon.

He's Got The Whole World

Starting pitch

Strum | Down up | Down up | Down up | Down up

He's got the whole world___ in His hands,___ He's got the whole world___ in His hands___ He's got the whole world___ in His hands,___ He's got the whole world in His hands.___

2. He's got the little bitsy baby. . . . 3. He's got you and me brother. . . . .

Hey Lolly

Starting pitch

Strum | Down up | Down up

Chorus Hey lol - ly, lol - ly, lol - ly, Hey lol - ly, lol - ly, lo.___

Hey lol - ly, lol - ly, lol - ly, Hey lol - ly, lol - ly, lo.___

C
1. Wake up in the mornin', sunny **and** bright
   G7
   Hey lolly, lolly lo.
   Looked in the mirror, got a terrible fright!
   C
   Hey lolly, lolly lo.
   C
2. I have a girl she's ten feet tall,
   G7
   Hey lolly, lolly lo.
   Sleeps on the floor with her feet in the hall,
   C
   Hey lolly, lolly lo.

[make up your own verses]

18

The F Chord

Master the following chord study:

Repeat until no time is lost in changing.

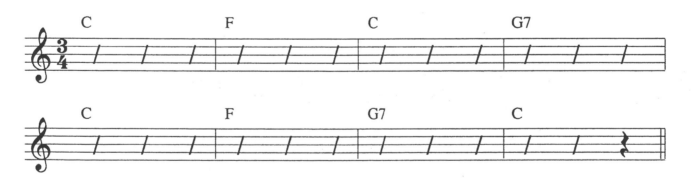

The C, F, and G7 chords are the principal chords in the key of C.

Santa Lucia

Yellow Rose Of Texas

Swanee River

Wildwood Flower

Starting pitch

Strum Down up Down up Down Down

C
I will twine with my ming - les of ra - ven black hair_____

G7   C

_____ with the ro - ses so red and the li - lies so fair,_____

G7   C

_____ The myr-tle so bright with its em - er - ald dew_____

F   C

_____ And the pale and the lead - er and eyes look so blue._____

G7   C

Our Boys Will Shine Tonight

Starting pitch

D7*

Strum Down up Down up Down Down

C
Our boys will shine to - night, our boys will shine.

F   C

Our boys will shine to - night, all down the line.

D7*   G7

C
Our boys will shine to - night, our boys will shine. When the

F   C

F   C   G7   C
sun goes down and the moon comes up, our boys will shine.

The Marine's Hymn

Camptown Races

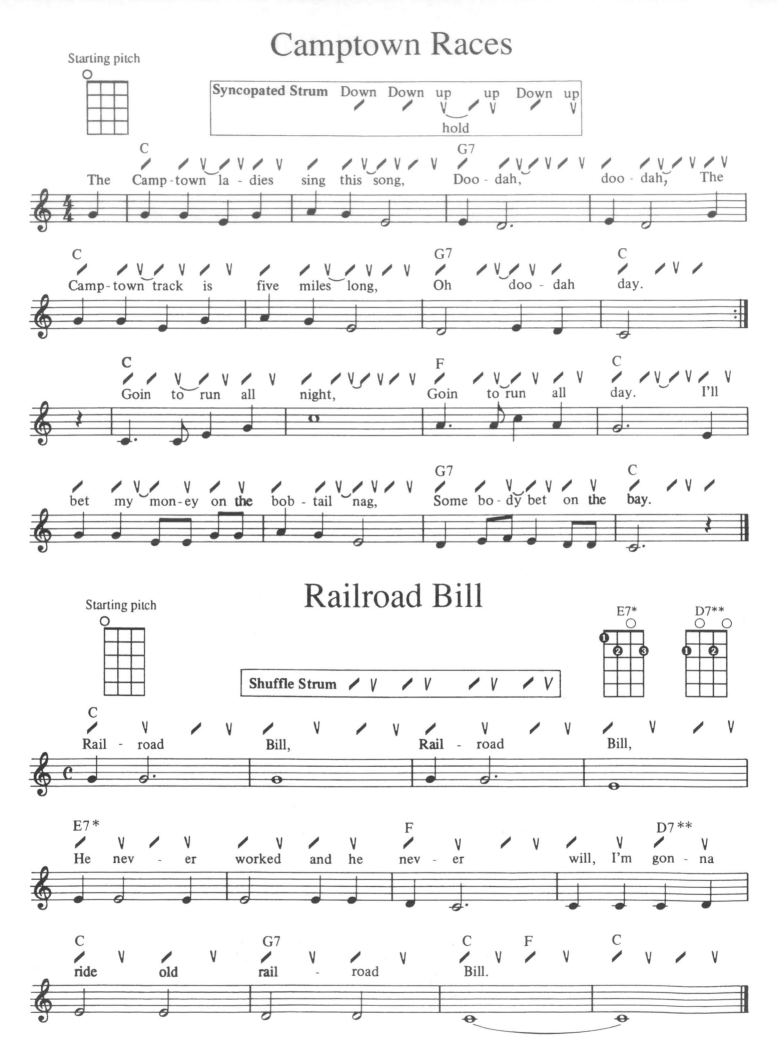

Railroad Bill

Every Time I Feel The Spirit

Starting pitch

Syncopated Strum Down Down up up Down up
hold

Chorus: Ev - ry time I feel the spirit **mov-in'** in my **heart** I will pray, ev' - ry
time I feel The spi - rit mov - 'in in my heart I will pray. Verse: U - pon the
moun-tain, when my Lord spoke, out of his mouth came fire and smoke; Look'd all a -
round me it looked so fine 'til I asked my Lord if all were mine.

Standing In The Need Of Prayer

Starting pitch

Shuffle Strum Down up Down up Down up Down up

Ain't my broth-er or my sis-ter but it's me, oh, Lord, stand-ing in the need of
prayer, Ain't my broth-er or my sis-ter but it's me, oh, Lord, stand-ing in the need of
prayer. It's me, it's me, oh, Lord, stand-ing in the need of
prayer, it's me, it's me, oh, Lord, stand-ing in the need of prayer

25

Two New Chords

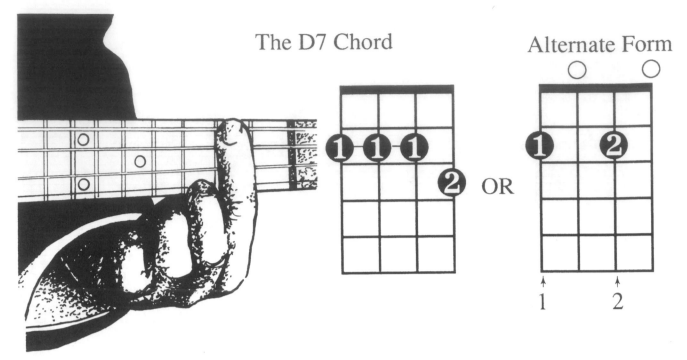

The D7 Chord

Alternate Form

OR

Play the following chord study:

C   D7   G7   C

(repeat)

The G Chord

The chords in the key of G are: G, C, and D7.

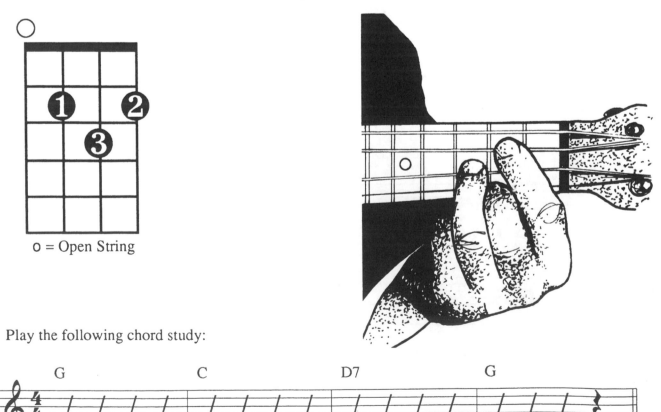

o = Open String

Play the following chord study:

G   C   D7   G

Aloha Oe
(Farewell To Thee)

Moonlight Bay

Go Tell It On The Mountain

Battle Hymn Of The Republic

2. I have seen Him in the watch fires of a hundred circling camps.
They have builded Him an altar in the evening dews and damps.
I have read His righteous sentence by the dim of flaring lamps,
His truth is marching on.

3. In the beauty of the lilies, Christ was born across the sea,
With a glory in His bosom that transfigures you and me;
As He died to make men holy, Let us die to make men free,
While God is marching on.

Away In A Manger

This Little Light Of Mine

Peace Like A River

All Through The Night

Blow, Ye Winds

The Wabash Cannonball

Down By The Riverside

2. I'm gonna join hands with everyone, etc.
3. I'm gonna put on my long white robe, etc.
4. I'm gonna talk with the **Prince of Peace, etc.**

She'll Be Coming Round The Mountain

The Gospel Train

2. The fare is cheap and all can go,
   The rich and poor are there;
   No second class aboard this train,
   No difference in the fare. Chorus

3. I hear that train a-comin',
   She sure is speedin' fast,
   So get your tickets ready
   And ride to heaven at last. Chorus

35

Chords In The Key Of D

The three primary chords in the key of D are: D, G, and A7.

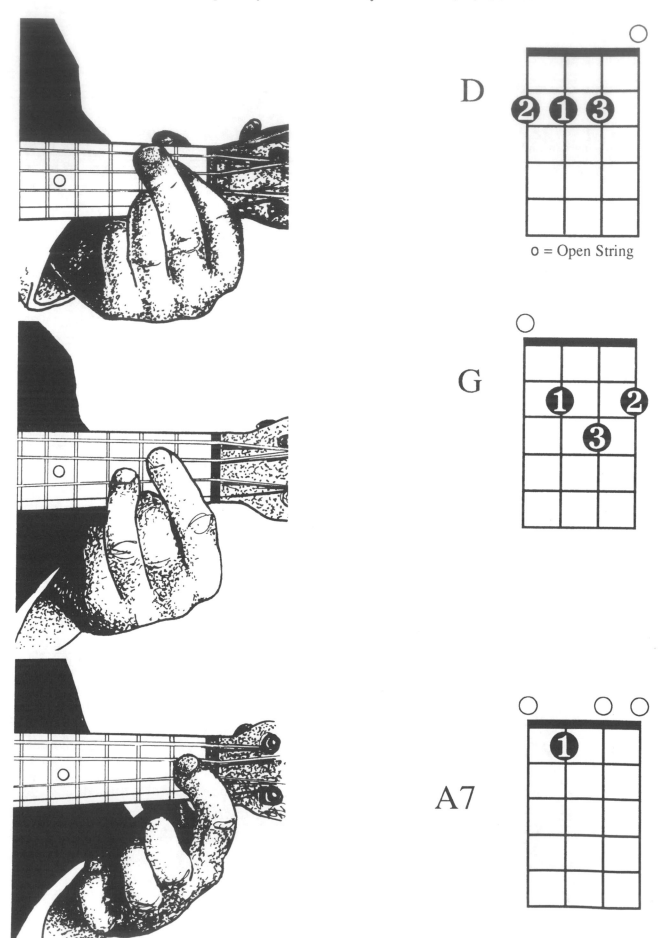

D

o = Open String

G

A7

She Wore A Yellow Ribbon

Starting pitch

Strum   Down   Down   up   Down   Down

American
Folk Song

Bright Tempo

A - round her hair, She wore a yel- low rib-bon; She wore it in the spring-time and in the month of May, And if you asked her why the heck she wore it, she wore it for her sol- dier boy who's far, far a - way. Far a-

Chorus: way, _____ far a - way _____ she wore it for her sol - dier boy who's far, far a - way. _____

D
But, in her heart, she has a secret passion
A7
She has it in the springtime, and in the month of May;
D
And if you asked her who is now her passion,
A7   **D**
She has it for a college man who's not so far away.
Chorus

When The Saints Go Marchin' In

Starting pitch

2. And when they gather 'round the throne.
3. And when they crown him **King** of kings
4. And on that Hallelujah day.

Streets Of Laredo

2. "Go fetch me a cup, a cup of cold water,
To cool my parched lips," the cowboy then said;
Before I returned, the spirit had left him
And gone to its Maker - the cowboy was dead.

3. We beat the drum slowly and played the fife lowly,
And bitterly wept as we bore him along;
For we all loved our comrade, so brave, young, and handsome,
We all loved our comrade although he'd done wrong.

Crawdad Song

The Girl I Left Behind Me

Starting pitch

Strum Down Rest Down up

D   G   A7   D

I am lone-some since I crossed the hill and o'er the moor and val - ley, such a

G   A7   D

heav - y thought my heart do fill since part - ing with my__ Las - sie. I__

                                             A7

seek no more the joy in life, for ech - oes but re - mind me how__

D   G   A7   D

swift the hours did pass a - way with the girl I left be - hind me.

Li'l Liza Jane

Starting pitch

Strum Down Rest Down up Down up Down up

D

I got a gal and you got none Li'l Liz - a Jane,

A7   D

I got a gal that calls me hon; Li'l Liz - a Jane.

D   G   D   G   D   A7

Chorus Oh E - liz - a, Li'l Liz - a Jane,

D   G   D   A7   D

Oh E - liz - a, Li'l Liz - a Jane.

40

Oh! Susanna

Come And Go With Me

Starting pitch
(down 1 octave)

2. There'll be singin' in that land   3. There'll be dancin' in that land.
4. There is freedom in that land   5. There is love in that land.

Frankie & Johnny

Starting pitch

42

Chords In The Key of F

The three primary chords in the key of F are: F, B♭, and C7.

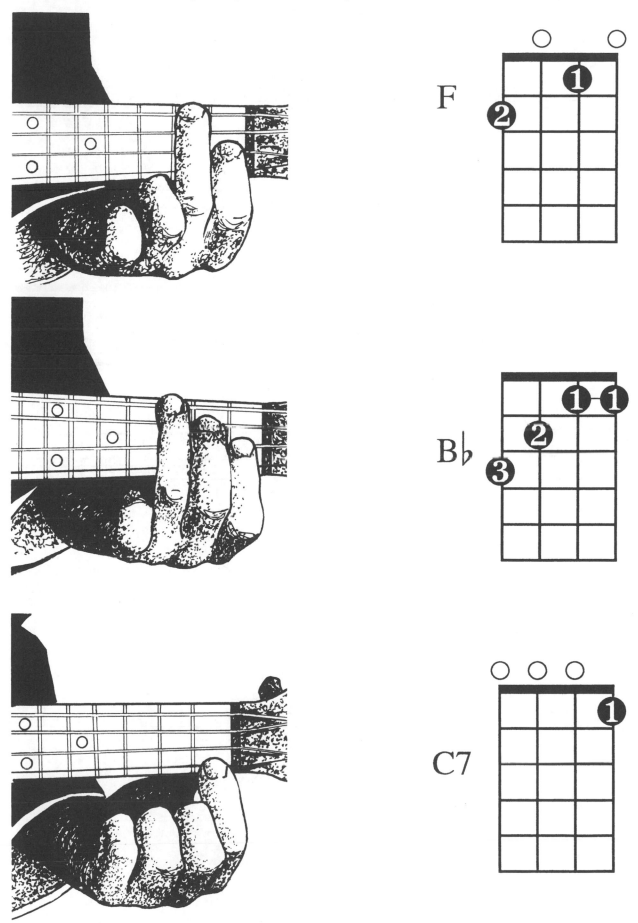

Juanita

2. When in thy dreaming moons like these shall shine again,
And daylight beaming prove thy dreams are vain,
Wilt thou not, relenting, for thine absent lover sigh?
In thy heart consenting to a prayer gone by?
Nita! Juanita! Let me linger by thy side!
Nita! Juanita! Be my own fair bride.

Swing Low, Sweet Chariot

Starting pitch

Strum: Down Down Down Down up
/ / / / V

2. When I get to glory, my voice I'll raise,
   Comin' for to carry me home,
   To sing a song of grateful praise,
   Comin' for to carry me home.

Starting pitch

Sweet By And By

Strum: Down Down up Down up Down up
/ / V / V / V

Gospel Song

F   Bb   F
/   /   /   V /V   /   V /   /V   /V   /   V
There's a   land that is fair — er than day,   and by

                    C7   F   Bb
/   /   V /V   /   V   /   /V/V   /   V   /   /   V /V   /   V
faith we can see it a — far,   for the Fa — ther waits o — ver the

F   C7   F   Bb   F
/   /V   /V   /   V   /   /   V /   /   V   /   /V /V
way,   To pre — pare us   a dwell — ing place there.

Chorus   F   C7   Bb   C7   F
/   V   / /V/V /   V   / /V/V /   V   /   /   V /V /   V / /V/V /   V
In the sweet by and by, We shall meet on that beau – ti – ful shore, In the

                Bb   F   C7   F
/   /V /V /   V   / /V /V /   V   /   /   V /V /   V / /V/
sweet   by and by, We shall meet on that beau – ti – ful shore.

            F   Bb   F   F   Bb   F
2. We shall sing on that beautiful shore   3. To our beautiful Father above
            C7   C7
The melodious songs of the blest;   We will offer our tribute of praise,
            F   Bb   F   F   Bb   F
And our spirits shall sorrow no more   For the glorious gift of his love
            C7   F Bb F   C7   F Bb F
Not a sigh for the blessing of rest.   And the blessings that hallow our days.

Chorus   *Chorus*

This Train

Starting pitch

Strum: Down Down up Down up Down up
/ / V / V / V

F
/ / V / V / V / / V / V / V / / V / V / V / / V / V / V
This Train is bound for glo — ry, This train. _____

/ / V / V / V / / V / V / V / / V / V / V / / V / V / V
This train is bound for glo — ry, This train. _____
(C7)

F
/ / V / V / V / / V / V / V / / V / V / V / / V / V / V
This train is bound for glo — ry, don't car-ry noth-in' but the right-eous and the ho — ly
(Bb)

F
/ / V / V / V / / V / V / V / / V / V / V / / V / V / V
This train is bound for glo — ry This train. _____
(Bb) (C7) (F)

Mary Ann

Starting pitch

Syncopated Strum: Down Down up   up Down up
/ / V / V / V
Hold

F
/ / V / V / V / / V / V / V / / V / V / V / / V / V / V
All day, all night Ma — ry Ann _____
(C7)

/ / V / V / V / / V / V / V / / V / V / V / / V / V / V
down by The sea — shore sift-ing sand _____
(F)

/ / V / V / V / / V / V / V / / V / V / V / / V / V / V
Ev — en lit — tle chil — dren love Ma — ry Ann, _____
(C7)

/ / V / V / V / / V / V / V / / V / V / V / / V / V / V
'cause she sings and dan — ces like No one can. _____
(F)

47

48

Fascination

CHORDS Needed:

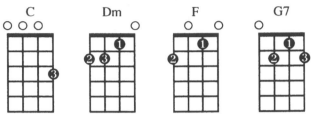

Starting pitch
(down 1 8ve)

Suggested Strum: Down Down Down up

Chinatown, My Chinatown

CHORDS Needed:

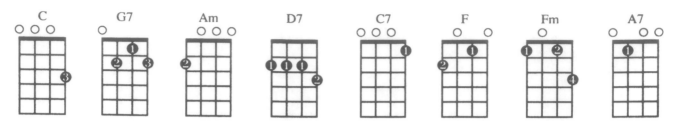

Starting pitch

Suggested Strum: | Down up Down up | up Down up |

C Chi - na - town, my Chi - na - town,_____ Where the lights are

G7 low,_____ Hearts that know no oth - er land,_____ **Am** **D7** Drift - ing

to and **G7** fro,_____ Dream - y, dream - y **C** Chi - na - town,_____

Al - mond **C7** eyes of **F** brown,_____ Hearts seem light **Fm** and

C life seems bright_____ **A7** In dream - y **D7** Chi - na **G7** - town. **C** _____

Ida, Sweet As Apple Cider

When Irish Eyes Are Smiling

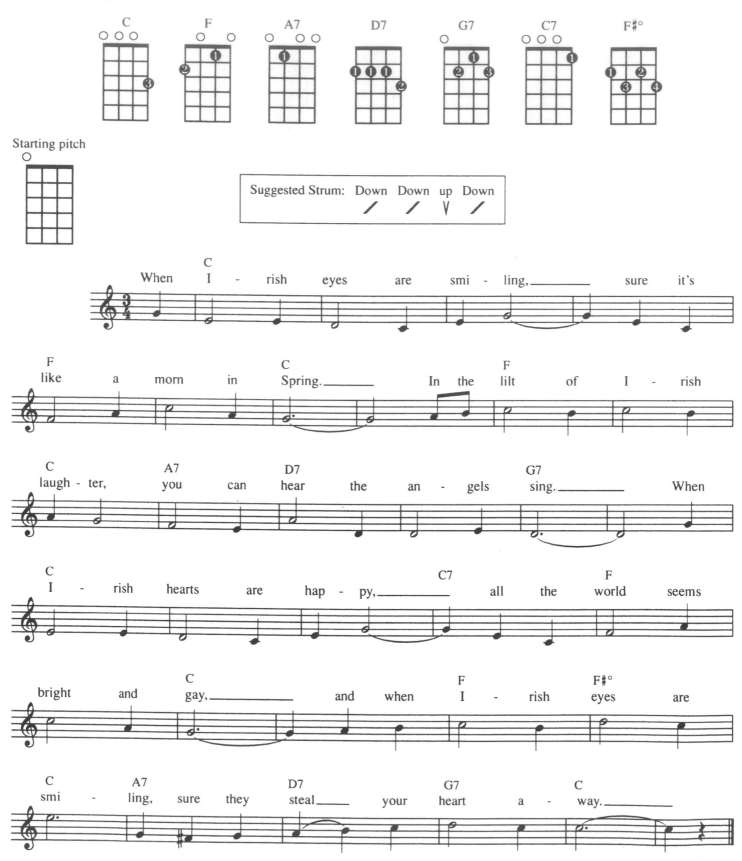

By the Light of the Silvery Moon

The Darktown Strutters' Ball

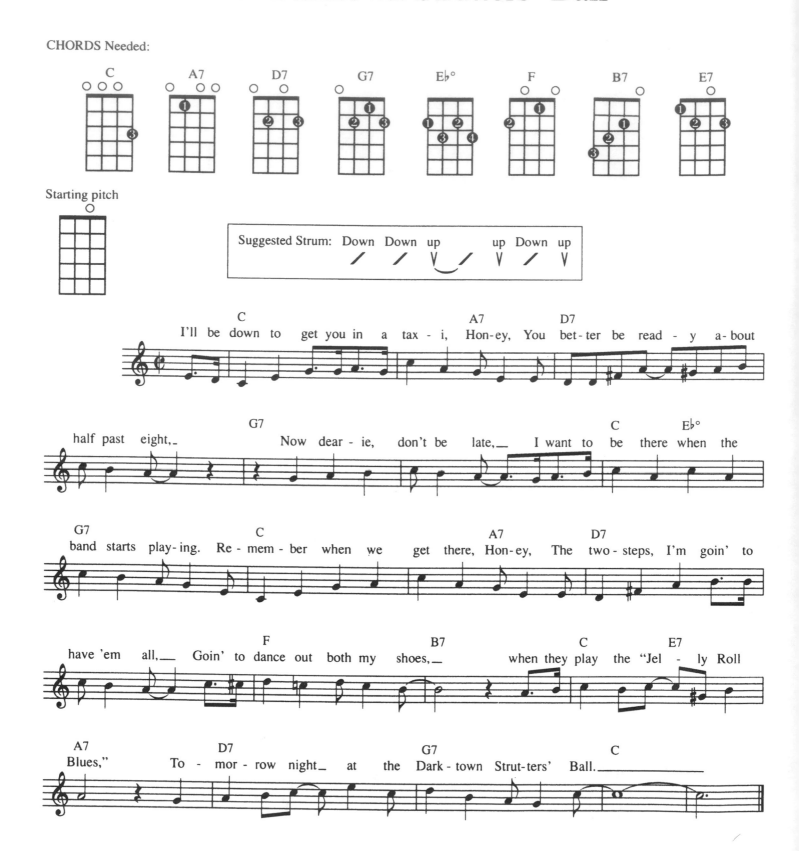

That's An Irish Lullaby

CHORDS Needed:

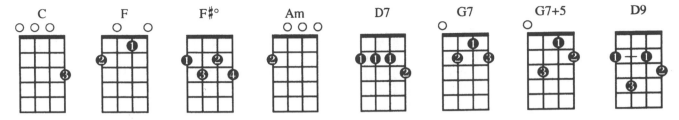

Starting pitch

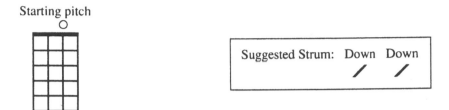

Suggested Strum: Down Down

Slowly

Too – ra - loo – ra - loo - ral,_____ Too – ra - loo – ra – li,

Too – ra - loo – ra - loo - ral,_____ Hush now, don't you cry!_____

Too – ra - loo – ra - loo - ral,_____ Too – ra - loo – ra – li,

Too – ra - loo – ra - loo - ral, That's an I - rish lul - la - by.

Meet Me In St. Louis, Louis

Dear Old Girl

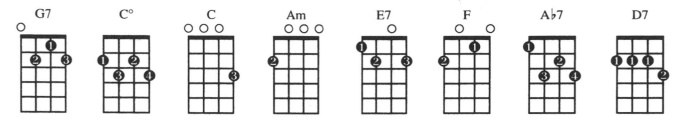

CHORDS Needed:

G7   C°   C   Am   E7   F   A♭7   D7

Starting pitch

Suggested Strum: Down Down up Down up Down

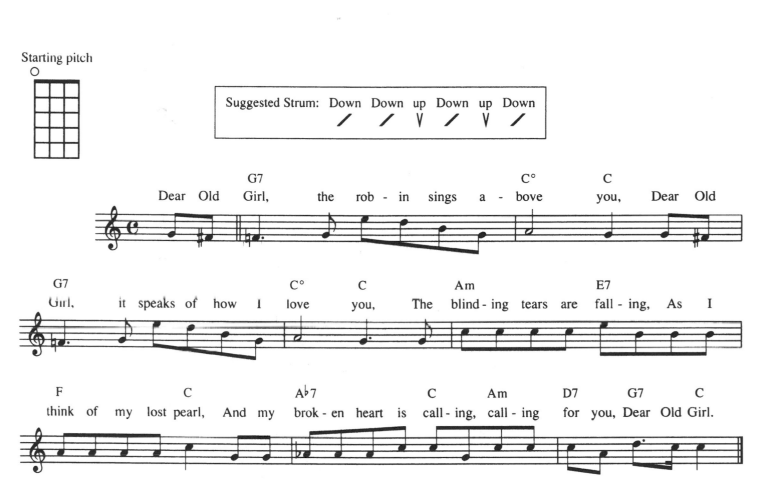

	G7		C°	C	
Dear Old	Girl,	the rob - in sings a - bove	you,	Dear	Old

G7		C°	C	Am	E7
Girl,	it speaks of how I love	you,	The blind - ing tears are fall - ing,	As	I

F	C	A♭7	C	Am	D7	G7	C
think of my lost pearl,	And my brok - en heart is	call - ing, call - ing	for you, Dear Old Girl.				

Key of G

In My Merry Oldsmobile

CHORDS Needed:

Starting pitch

Suggested Strum: Down Down up Down

D7   G   E7   A7
Come a - way with me Lu - cile_____ In my mer - ry

                      D7
Olds - mo - bile._____ Down the road of life we'll fly, Au - to - mo -

G   D°   D7   G   E7
bubb - ling you and I. To the church we'll swift - ly steal,_____

        A7   D7
___ Then our wed - ding bells will peal,_____ You can go as far as you

G   Em   A7   D7   G
like with me, In my mer - ry Olds - mo - bile._____

58

Shine On Harvest Moon

CHORDS Needed:

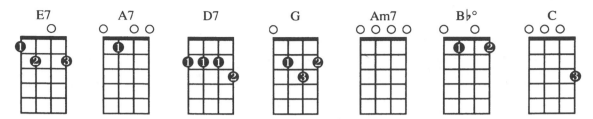

Starting pitch

Suggested Strum: Down Down up   up Down up

E7   A7
Oh, shine on, shine on har-vest moon,_____ up in the sky.

D7   G   Am7   B♭°   G
I ain't had no lov - in' since Jan-u-ar-y, Feb-ru-ar-y, June or Ju-ly.___

E7   A7
Snow time ain't no time to stay_____ out-doors and spoon. So

D7   G   C   G
shine on, shine on har - vest moon, for me and my gal.___

59

The Sidewalks of New York
[East Side, West Side]

CHORDS Needed:

Wait Till The Sun Shines, Nellie

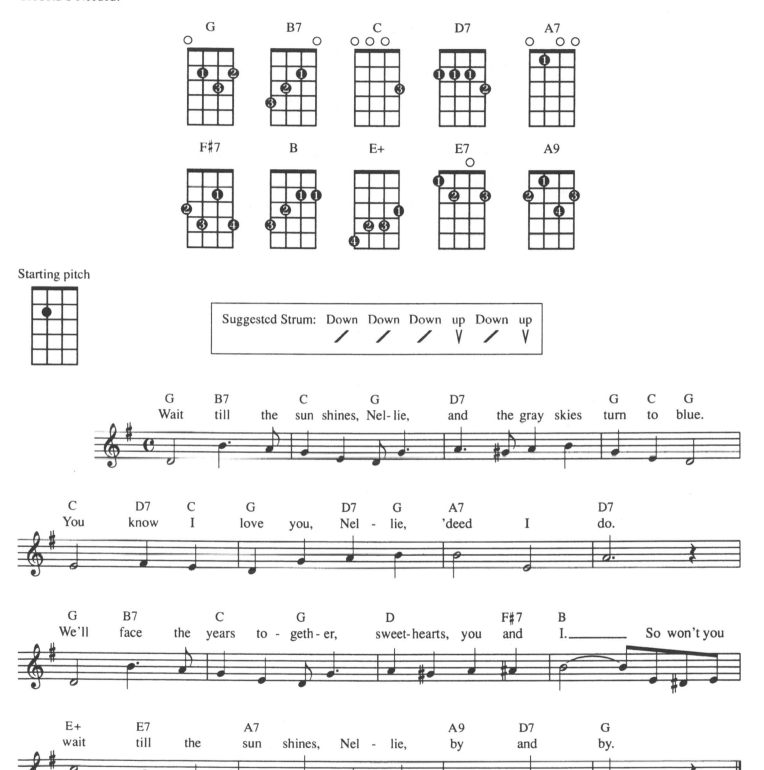

Down By The Old Mill Stream

While Strolling Through The Park One Day

Bill Bailey, Won't You Please Come Home?

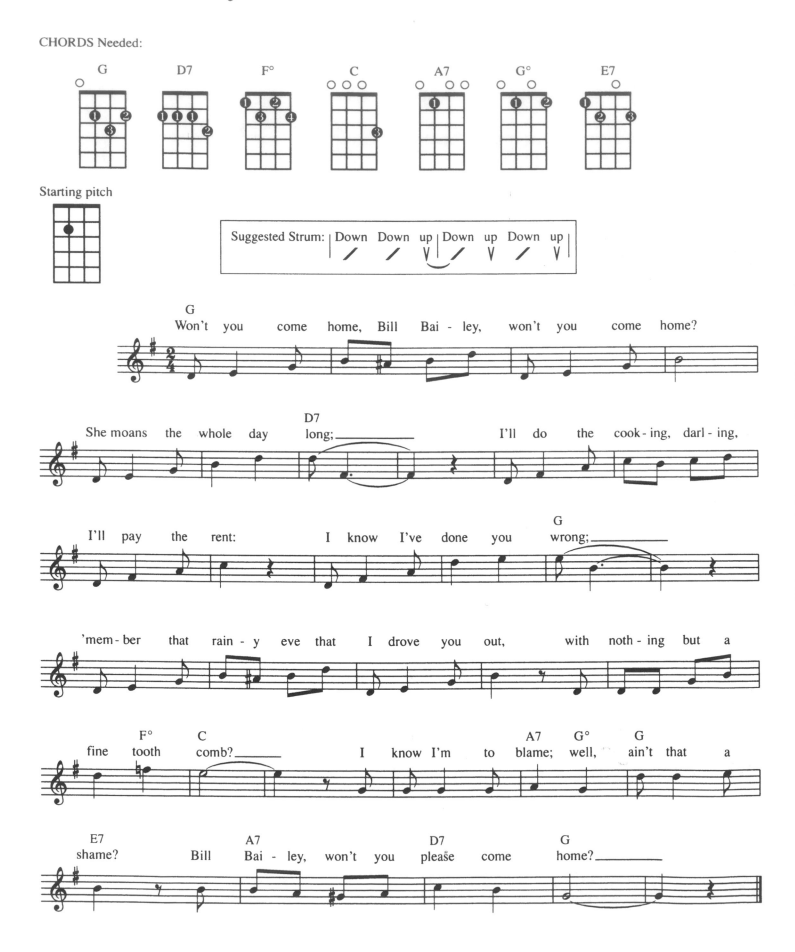

For Me And My Gal

Oh, You Beautiful Doll

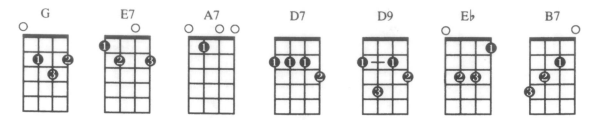

CHORDS Needed:

I Wonder Who's Kissing Her Now

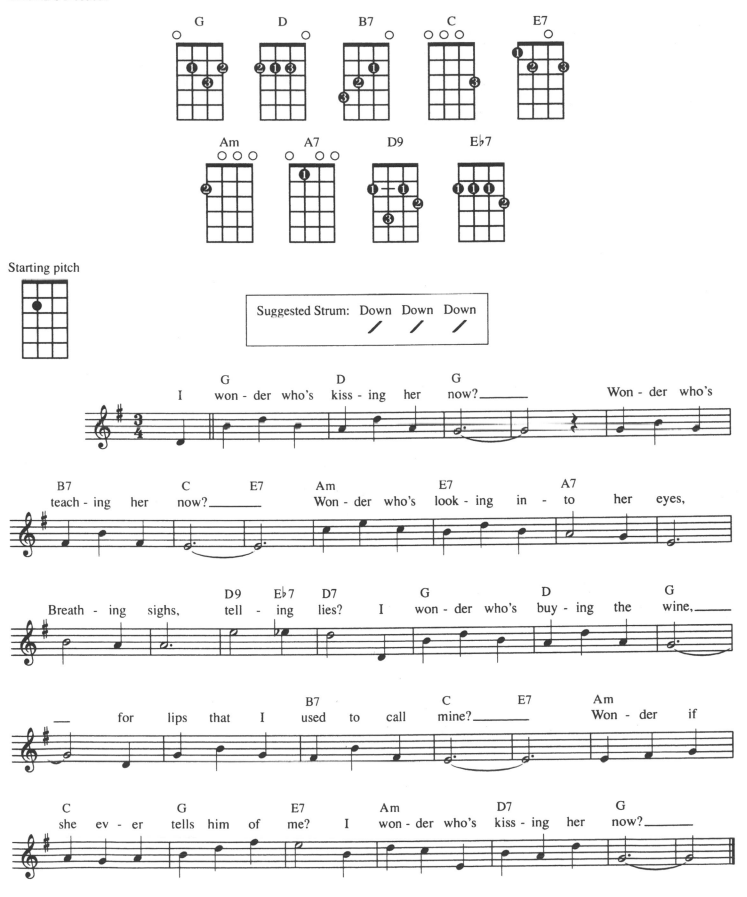

I Want A Girl

CHORDS Needed:

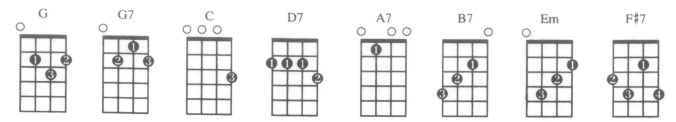

Starting pitch

Suggested Strum: Down Down up Down up Down up

| G | G7 | C | | G | D7 | G |
I want a girl just like the girl that mar - ried dear old Dad.

C | G | A7 | D7 | A
She was a girl and the on - ly girl that Dad - dy ev - er had._____ A

G | B7 | Em | B7 (F#7) D7
good old fash-ioned girl with heart so true, one who loves no-bod - y else but you.

G | G7 | C | | G | D7 | G
I want a girl just like the girl that mar - ried dear old Dad.

68

Poor Butterfly

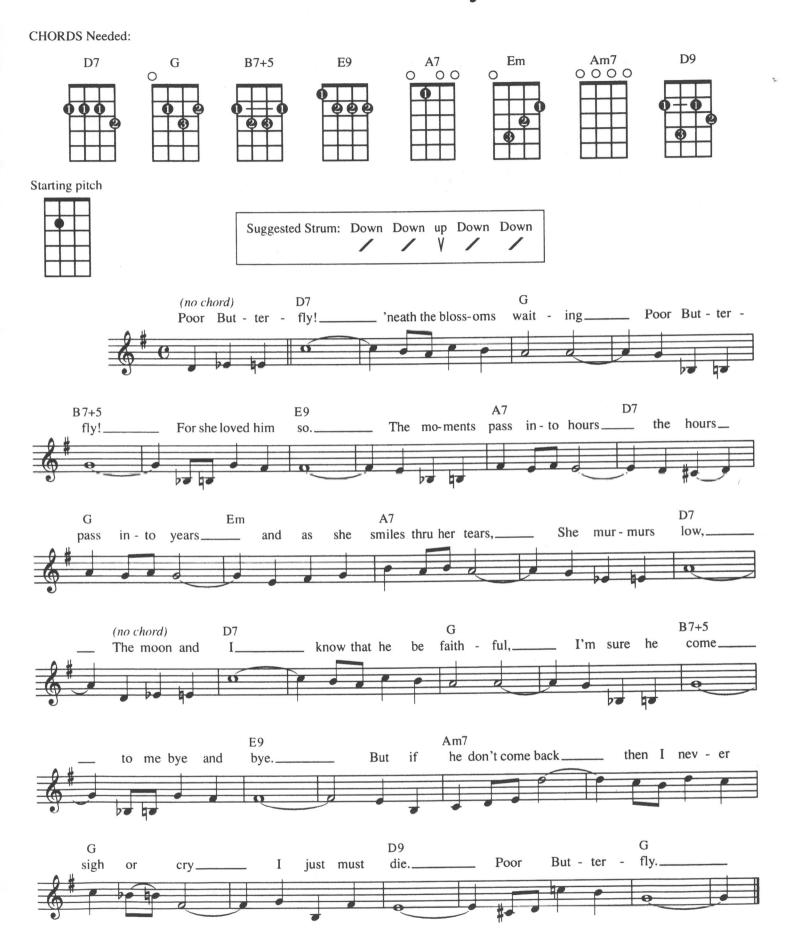

When You And I Were Young, Maggie

CHORDS Needed:

Starting pitch

Suggested Strum: Down Down up Down Down up

F
I___ wan- dered to- day to the hill, Mag-gie, To watch the___ scene be -

C7   F   Bb   F   C7
low,   The___ creek and the old rust-y mill, Mag-gie, where we sat in the long,___ long a -

F   Bb   Gm7   F   C   G7
go.   The green grove is gone from the hill,   Mag-gie, Where first the dai - sies___

C   C7   F   Bb   F   C7   F
sprung; The   old rust-y mill is___ still Maggie, since you and___ I were_ young.

70

Hello! Ma Baby

CHORDS Needed:

Starting pitch

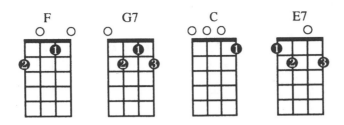

Suggested Strum: Down up   up Down Down

F
Hel - lo! ma ba - by, Hel - lo! ma hon - ey, Hel - lo! ma rag - time

gal,   C7 Send me a kiss by wire,   F Ba - by   E7 my heart's on

C7 fire!   F If you re - fuse me, Hon - ey, you'll lose me,   G7 Then you'll be left a -

lone, Oh, ba - by,   C7 Tel - e - phone and tell me I'm your   F own._____

71

Melody of Love

Alexander's Ragtime Band

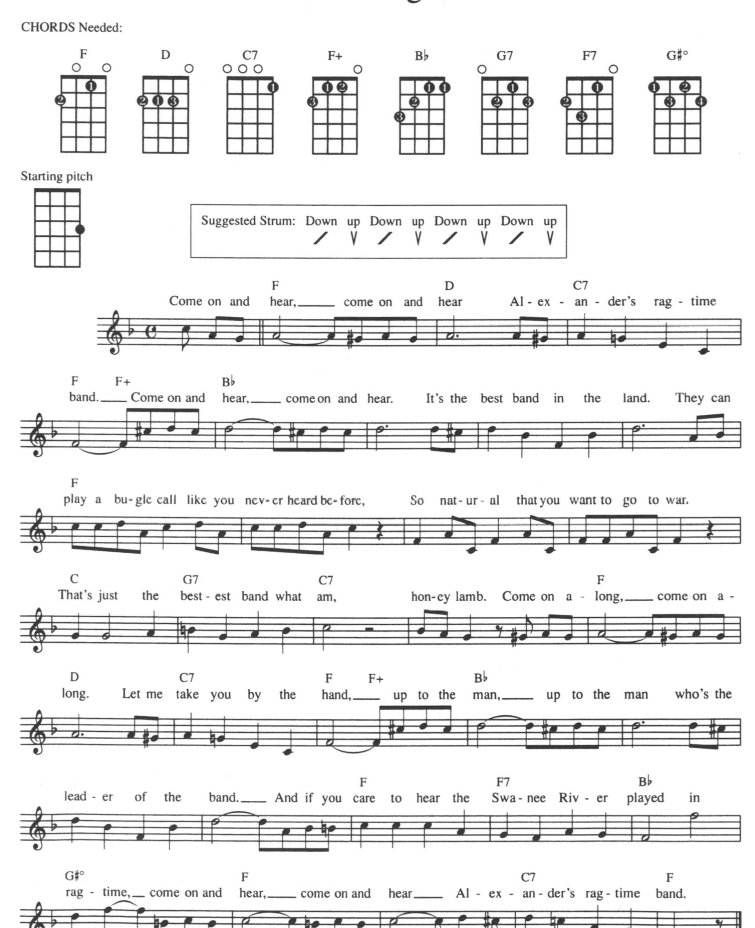

After the Ball

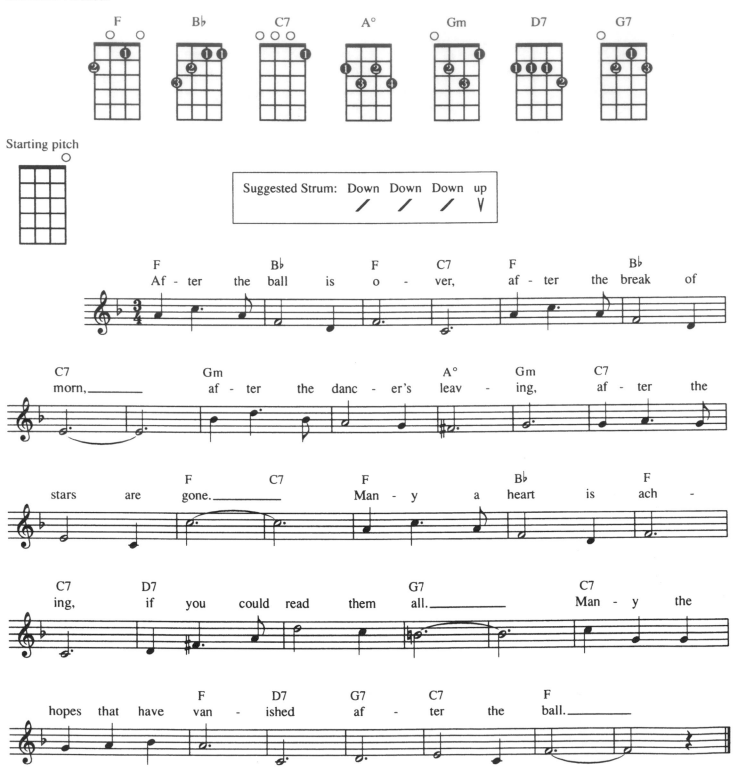

I Love You Truly

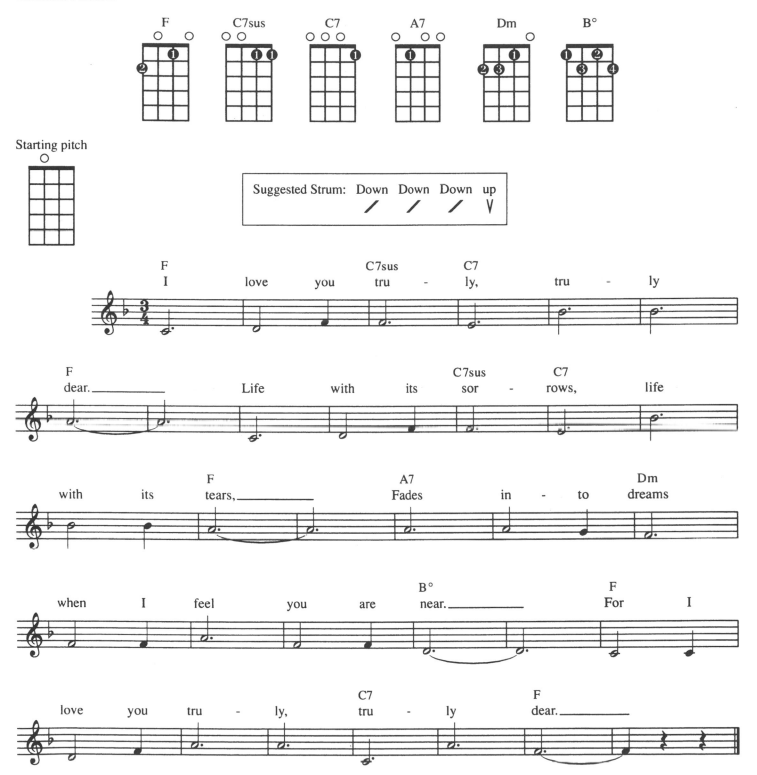

You're A Grand Old Flag

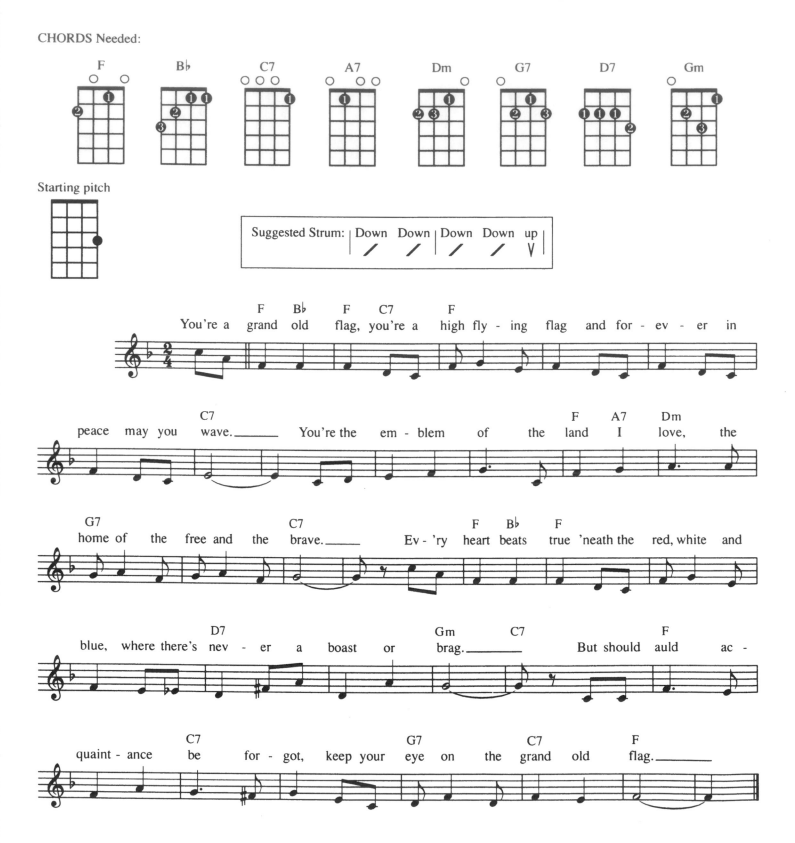

Bicycle Built For Two

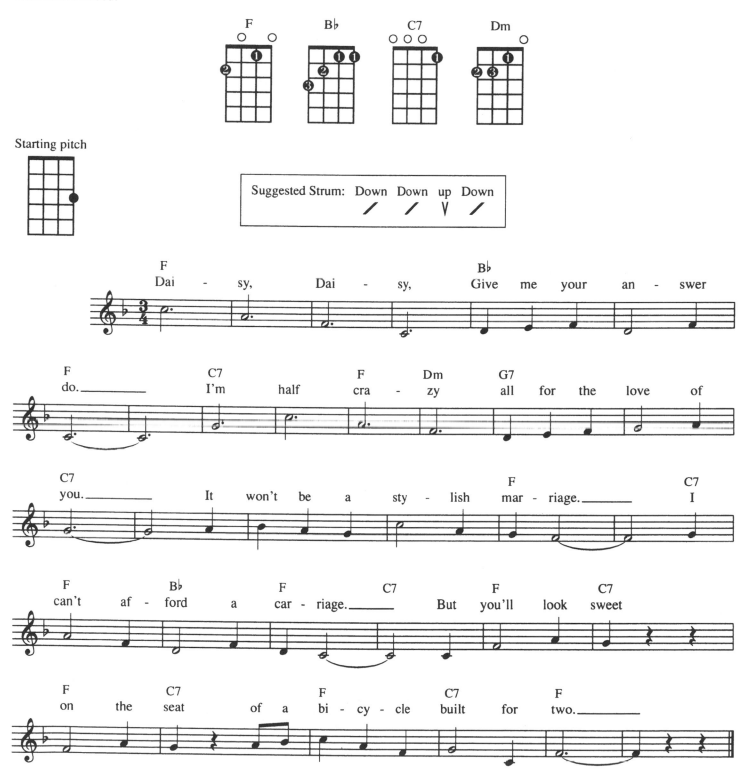

Alabama Jubilee

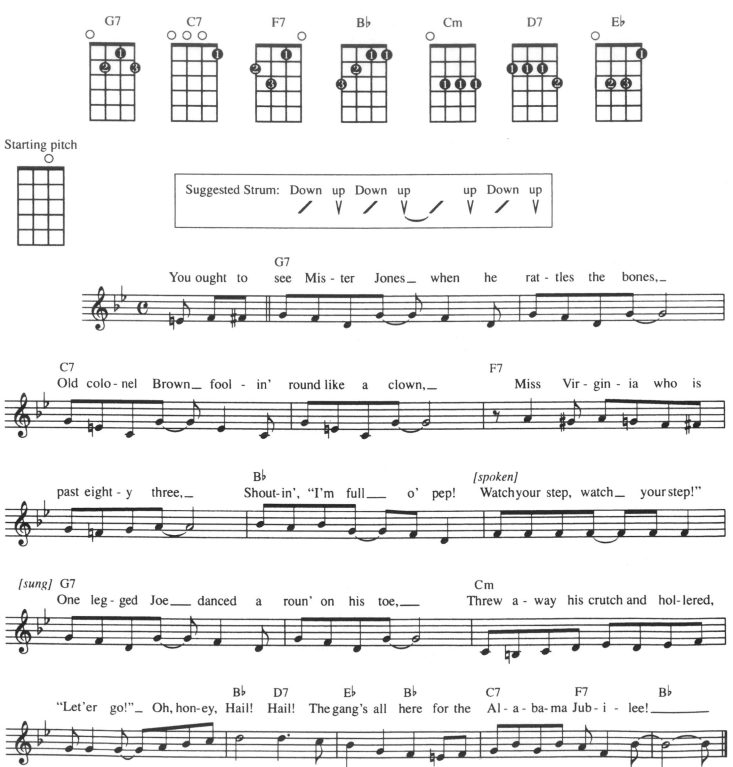

Sweet Rosie O'Grady

Peg O' My Heart

CHORDS Needed:

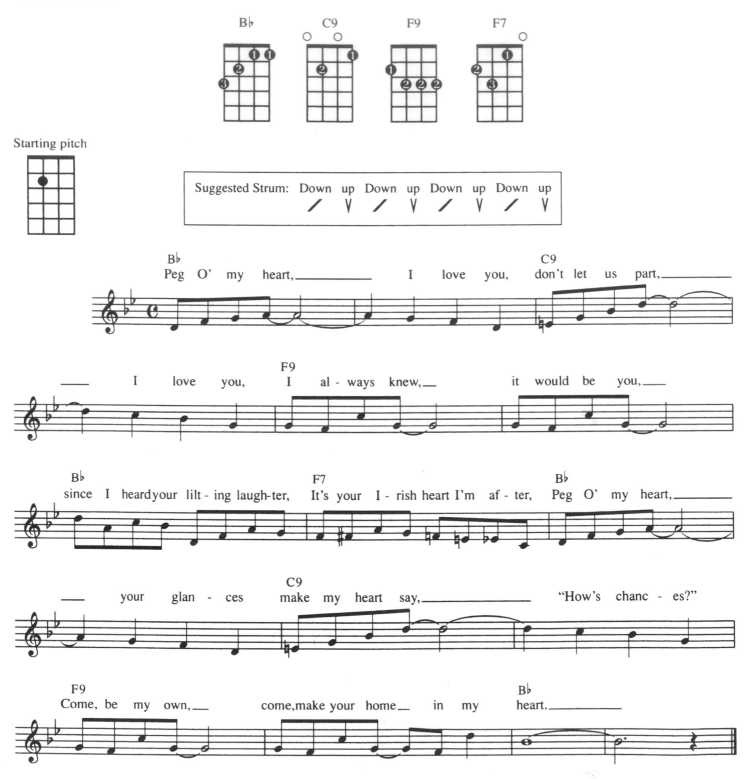

Ballin' The Jack

CHORDS Needed:

In The Good Old Summertime

CHORDS Needed:

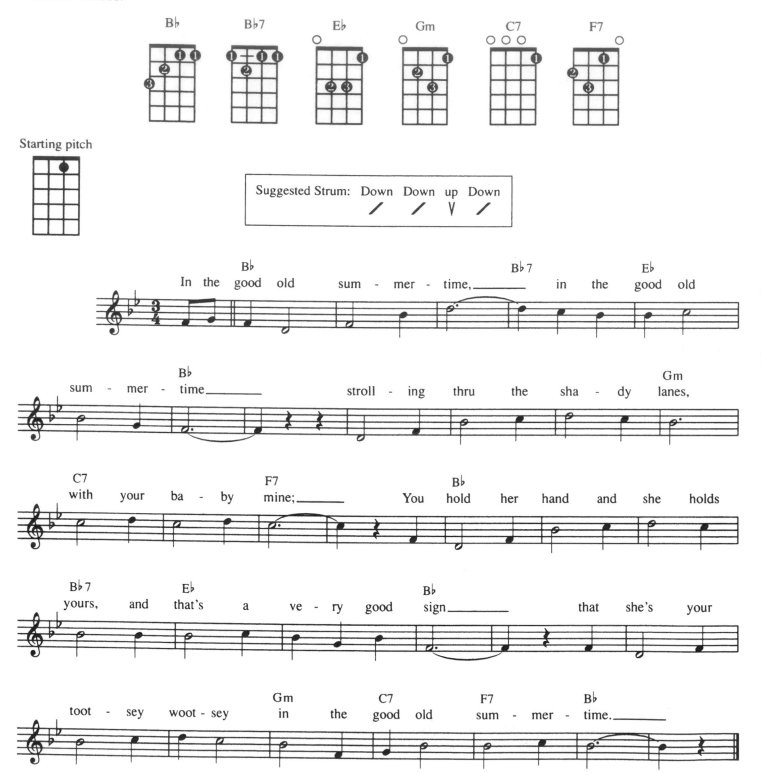

82

The Yankee Doodle Boy

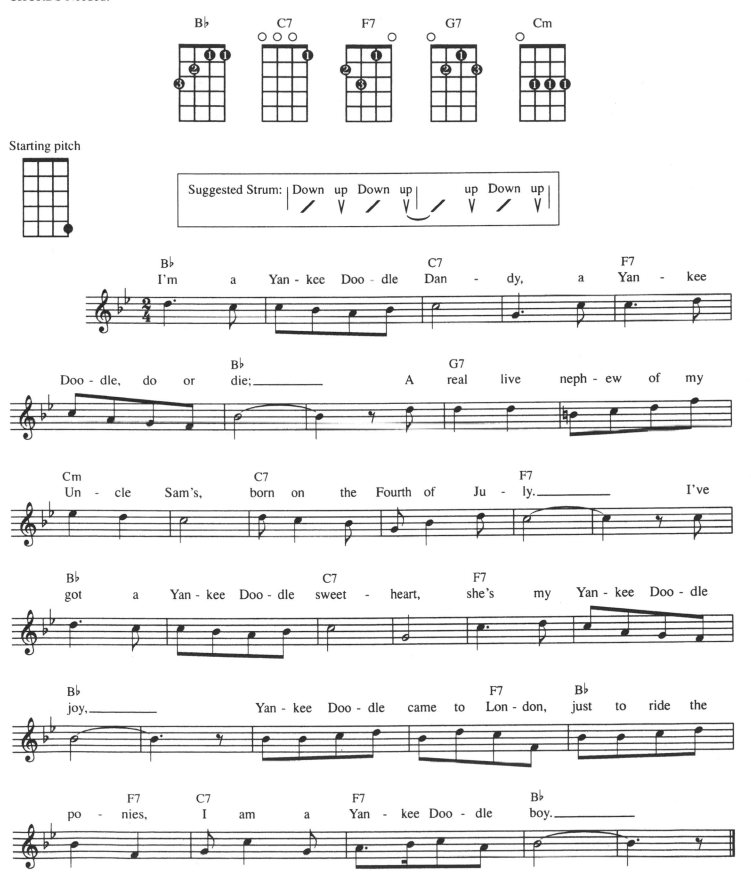

My Gal Sal

My Wild Irish Rose

CHORDS Needed:

Starting pitch

Give My Regards To Broadway

Take Me Out To The Ballgame

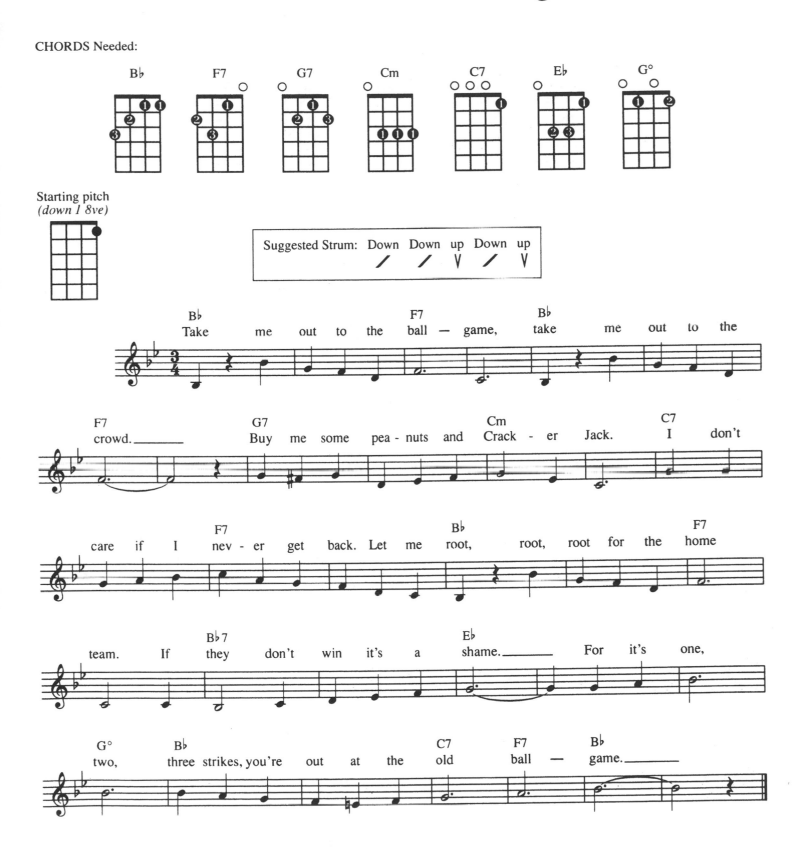

Let Me Call You Sweetheart

The Blue Bells of Scotland

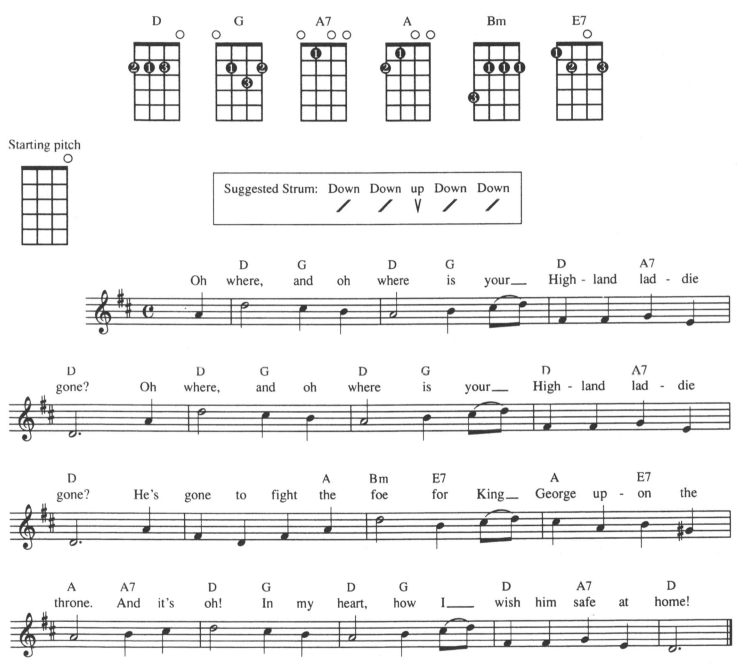

CHORDS Needed:

Starting pitch

Suggested Strum: Down Down up Down Down

Oh where, and oh where is your___ High - land lad - die gone?

Oh where, and oh where is your___ High - land lad - die gone?

He's gone to fight the foe for King___ George up - on the throne.

And it's oh! In my heart, how I___ wish him safe at home!

Over the River and Through the Woods

CHORDS Needed:

Beautiful Dreamer

CHORDS Needed:

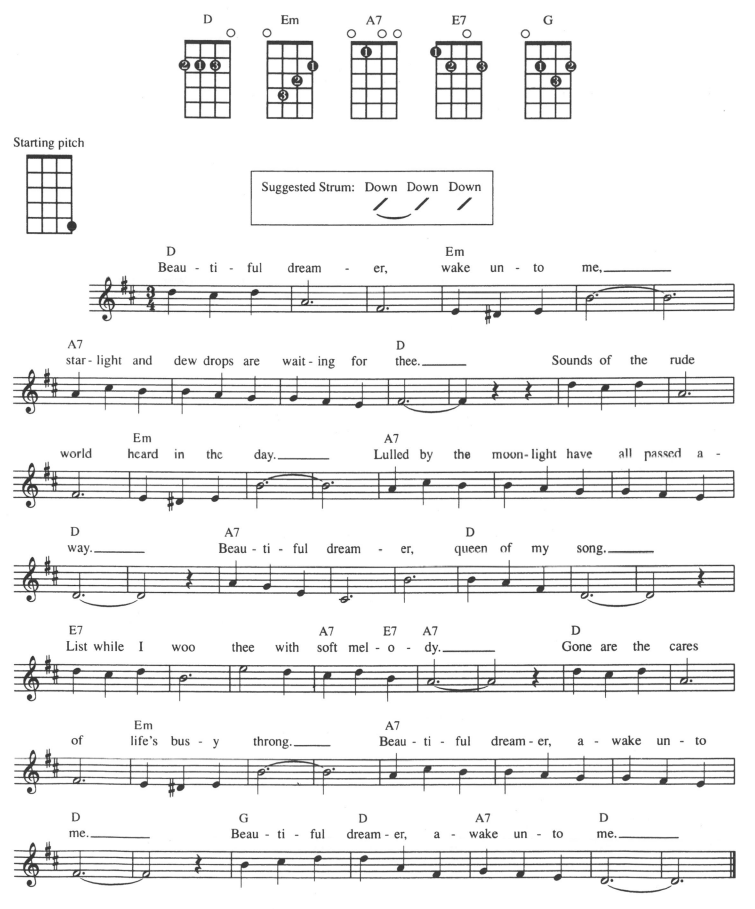

Pretty Baby

My Melancholy Baby

CHORDS Needed:

Starting pitch

Suggested Strum: Down up Down up Down Down up

D	B7+5	B7	Em

Come to me, my mel-an-chol-y ba - by, cud-dle up and don't be blue;

A7	E7	A7	D	A7

All your fears are fool-ish fan-cy, may be, you know, dear, that I'm in love with you.

D	B7+5	B7	Em

Ev - 'ry cloud must have a sil - ver lin - ing, wait un - til the sun shines through,

G	G♯°	D	B7	Em	A7	D

Smile my hon-ey dear, while I kiss a-way each tear, or else I shall be mel-an-chol-y too.

93

Basic Uke Chord Chart

MAJOR Chords

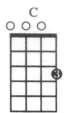 C   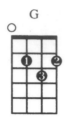 F   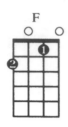 G   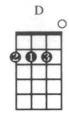 D   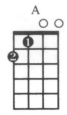 A   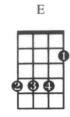 E

 B♭   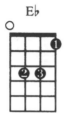 E♭   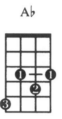 A♭   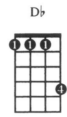 D♭   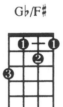 G♭/F♯   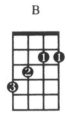 B

MINOR Chords

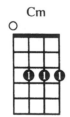 Cm   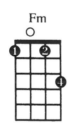 Fm   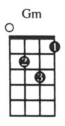 Gm   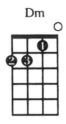 Dm    Am   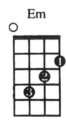 Em

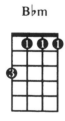 B♭m   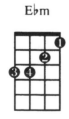 E♭m   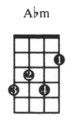 A♭m   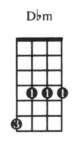 D♭m   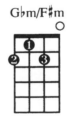 G♭m/F♯m   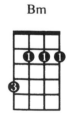 Bm

SEVENTH Chords

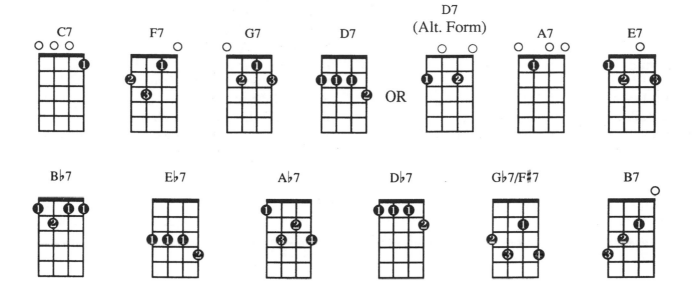

C7 F7 G7 D7 D7 (Alt. Form) OR A7 E7

Bb7 Eb7 Ab7 Db7 Gb7/F#7 B7

DIMINISHED Chords

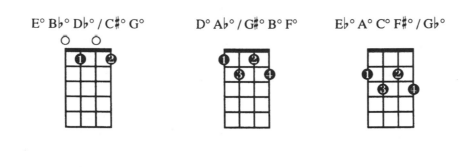

E° Bb° Db° / C#° G°   D° Ab° / G#° B° F°   Eb° A° C° F#° / Gb°

AUGMENTED Chords

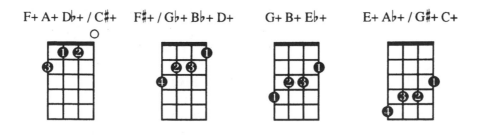

F+ A+ Db+ / C#+   F#+ / Gb+ Bb+ D+   G+ B+ Eb+   E+ Ab+ / G#+ C+

For complete Photo/Diagram Chord Listing see

Mel Bay's Ukulele Chord Book (MB 93269)

Index Of Songs